October for Idas

*O*ctober for *I*das

Star Black

PAINTED LEAF PRESS
NEW YORK CITY

Book design by Mary Carlson

LIBRARY OF CONGRESS CATALOGING-IN-PUBLICATION
Black, Star
    October for Idas /Star Black
        p.   cm.
    ISBN 0-9651558-1-1
    I. Titles.
PS3552.L34134028   1997
811' .54--dc21
                                   96-45638
                                       CIP

CONTENTS

Epigraph

90. Marpessa. Another maiden who declined Apollo's love was Marpessa.[1] She is called by Homer "the fair-ankled daughter of Evenus."

> The god Apollo from the heaven of heavens
> Her mortal sweetness through the air allured ; [2]

but Idas, "that was strongest of men that were then on earth," [1] carried her off, assisted by Poseidon who gave him a winged chariot. Her father Evenus vainly tried to catch up with the fleeing lovers; but Apollo found them in Messene, and wrested the maiden away. Then Jupiter, while the lovers were engaged in combat, separated them, saying, " Let her decide."

> They three together met ; on the one side,
> Fresh from diffusing light on all the world
> Apollo ; on the other without sleep
> Idas, and in the midst Marpessa stood.
> Just as a flower after drenching rain,
> So from the falling of felicity
> Her human beauty glowed, and it was new ;
> The bee too near her bosom drowsed and dropped.[2]

According to the story as romantically told by the English poet Phillips, first spoke Apollo. The god told her that he dreaded that one so fair should ever taste of sorrow and death ; how, if she lived with him, she should bide

> In mere felicity above the world
> In peace alive and moving, where to stir
> Is ecstasy, and thrilling is repose,[2]

immortal, scattering joy without intermission, lighting the world, bringing bliss to struggling men and sorrowing women, dispelling shadows and shadowy fear.

Then Idas, humbly, —

> "After such argument what can I plead?
> Or what pale promise make? Yet since it is
> In women to pity rather than to aspire,
> A little will I speak."

---

[1] Iliad, 9, 561 ; Apollodorus, 1, 7, § 8.   [2] Stephen Phillips, Marpessa.

And he tells her simply that he *loves* her, — loves her not only for her beauty, but

> " Because Infinity upon thee broods;
> And thou art full of whispers and of shadows; — "

and because her voice is music, her face mystery beyond his power to comprehend;

> " O beauty lone and like a candle clear
> In this dark country of the world! Thou art
> My woe, my early light, my music dying."

And Marpessa? —

> As he was speaking, she with lips apart
> Breathed, and with dimmer eyes leaned through the air
> As one in dream, and now his human hand
> Took in her own; and to Apollo spoke, —

saying that she knew how sweet it might be forever with a god to aid suffering men and women and " gild the face that from its dead looks up"; but still she feared immortality, for, though dying not, she must grow old, and her god lover would tire of her when once her youth was faded. And as for that " existence without tears for evermore " which he promised, —

> " Yet I being human, human sorrow miss.
> The half of music, I have heard men say,
> Is to have grieved."

To sorrow she was born. It is out of sadness that men have made this world beautiful. If she chooses Idas, then they two will prosper together, grow old together, and last descend into the " natural ground," and " leave behind a wholesome memory on the earth."

> When she had spoken, Idas with one cry
> Held her, and there was silence; while the god
> In anger disappeared. Then slowly they,
> He looking downward, and she gazing up,
> Into the evening green wandered away.

91. Clytie.[1] In the story of Clytie the conditions are reversed. She was a water-nymph and in love with Apollo, who made her

[1] Ovid, Metam. 4, 256–270.

October for Idas

Prologue

TAILGATING DIEBENKORN

It's time to leave "I" out of my work for five years,
remove the clock from the room. Charged daylight leers,
lances the throttled stratosphere, demanding the "alas" fears
inspire to drop off. A thick white-out deletes sighs: many careers
are shaken by this onslaught of omission. Atavistic as a chandelier
left aglow in the New Minimalism of interior design, an old chandelier,
old as the "I", "I" old, Io, the "I" must now go, crated and placed to the rear

of the foam-chip-sealed late-C'hing porcelain bowl in the basement near
the gilted oval mirror, a Victorian toad, and sepia photographs of dear
ones, wrapped carefully in tissue paper and locked in files for fear
of further disintegration, their empty metal frames now clear
of persons in costumes, retrieved, hung bare in the severe
white, minimal L-room where a presence sleeps in mere
flesh, while the raw-silk daylight calls "over here."

COUNTRY LIFE

Suddenly, a sandwiched breeze, curtailed by the Tree
of Heaven, a weedy determination flushed by pea-green
tufts of droopy blossoms, flopping like push-pinned bouquets
viewed through the shard of a glass bottle ground down by the sea,
urges, not me, but a silent surreal phantom outdoors into the comely
noon, scoured like a white sheet on a washing board, to find more relief
from the rectangular yawn of a hall, where nails invite decor. Loose seams,

unraveled by July, lower their bodice. Primavera escapes. Cows notice, lean
into the thin gravel roads, block cars, umbrella the spiders. Cicadas beat
their rumbly music through grass-blade lawns, frumped by the heat,
which stumbles like a drunkard toward shade. Unkempt plans keep
losing things, labors clumped like damp beach towels in a heap.
Nothing is strange. All ululates, skin a sin savored by priests
who are absent, sequestered, in heavens without trees.

GRRR

Some painters mad at Pop Art say
billboards with pink lipstick in a disarray
of slashed blondes work about as well as hairspray
on a mountain, that back in the beginning, in the heyday
of early abstraction, there was a genuine purity to painting, a
raw nerve, a tradition, before the crazy art world got carried away
with news clips and appropriation; that talented painters working today

exist on the edge of recognition, are not the names repetitively displayed
in market publications, but those few who carry on, quietly, unfazed
by the burbling commotion, in homage to Held, Kandinsky, Monet,
or Kenneth Noland (the list lengthens as if the sun's lancing rays
find no horizon but seep endlessly into the amethyst vales,
avoiding the slate dusk, the forked shadows of Man Ray,
his darkroom inventions, for bales of russet hay.)

Portrait of Steve

KUUSISTO IS BACK

I

The Czar's doctors are coming
and they like Coca-Cola.
They daydream leeches memorize historical dates.
The smell of shoe polish makes them brainy, misunderstood.
They need mothering that precedes language.
Their upstate dolor navigates deserts without compasses.
Addicted to sensation, they are post-taboo
but earnest at parties with mountains.
Ancient Arabs, too, openly expressed their own strengths.
Example: they were born on Venus.
The Czar's doctors hate
the hubbub of rote work, self-actualization, jugglers.
The best of them fall out of love.
Such folk, given a little room, encourage everyone.

II

The talking lap-top pleased the voodoo cabbie,
the business of writing, predatory in the coldest of months.
Skinny thawed street water played
a hand in who might knock,
the ducks in Italy, ravenous.
Puccini should be roaming the troubled elk
that butt heads with everyone,
the great hairy arctic creatures starving for sex with a petite girl.
Trouble is, advice in an Ithaca cafe is crazy as Strindberg,
the Finnish cuisine: *fin de siècle*,
yet, the logical outgrowth of living will get through cold hands,
Olga's tireless January.

III

Her spirits, mercifully, have headphones,
one primary goal—
dark spells and the world of astrology.
She is a beautiful girl, nice hair; we're not talking about his aunt.
Does she have people
to navigate sudden blindness?
The closet blew right through her head.
The cab races with special emphasis into stained glass.

IV

Tilted up or down, the sons of Homer
transmitted something grand
that fascinated Edgar's "hypnogogic state."
Benighted in a vast industrial room, the railway stations
shared that peculiar blankness that comes
to Barnum's center ring—
a palpable discrimination, a far-off look,
aspects of considerations or towering sunbeams.
A new scale in the coffee warehouse also shared the empty air,
the cathedral unaware, between walking and sleep.
Electric and shabby, their "one talent" gnostic,
they functioned historically as pedigree,
devised by Egyptian priests,
recalling whole books upon command.
Tiresias, Chaplin, with all seriousness, the templars infuse
the captioned savants The Lord opens.

GOING BLIND

I

Out there, behind the locomotive,
red veins, only inches away,
"contriving not to conclude against a wall of stone,"
ignite tiny fires in my head: the power to dream
in the primeval campground, pupils dilated with atropine
and the quick white feet of light.

The eye wants away. There is no away.
The retinal forest divides the doctor's face,
ecclesiastic, edgy.
A firmament vanishes during these exams,
and the desert noon empties beyond carpentry.
I am unimprovable, metallic, conclusive.
The skull matures and the very sunrise concedes.

In the oculist's chair,
the doctors talk in tones,
to "problemize" what was once Victorian.
The whalebone corset keeps upright the drugged.
Under glass, in a long black room, bandaged, et cetera,
borderline manners are a brand of currency.
The doctors like martial music,
befogged, vertiginous.

II

In the great Prado,
Velázquez hangs behind ropes,
in a sprawl, in oceans of mud.
The obscure cosmology of the telephone book,
its trajectory of lines and color, is also
thwarted by guards,
the print a microscopic souvenir,
a tilted cup of sand.

Swatting hornets in the Prado light,
dancing for Kali in the twin worlds of appearance and disappearance,
I turn in the prismatic veil,
and the oval skylights break up the world.
Ganesa whirls slowly through the cathedral to Goya,
bowing to the fetlock of a painted horse.
The Spanish docent describes
the elephant dance of light, the flapping windmill of man.

What is the color of water,
the cataract on the lake? The juice of carrots?
I am a noisy plaything in a tree full of starlings.
Night after night, thought wakes from an afternoon nap.
A Finnish poem arrives,
weary of the submariner's ballet.

III

A cobweb, and hobbling playmates
have no idea when the elders have gone.
The mooseheads and wind-up Victrolas terrify
the boyish eternity, wrapped in an immense, raccoon coat.
I play at my grandmother's calling from the other side,
a radio announcer, reciting lists.

The streetcars of Helsinki
have ether eyes,
a population in the black Finnish woods.
Snow comes, livid, to quiet the sheep.
It nurses shreds from a broom,
the trolley mystics in the sullen fire
flitting the curiosities of public conveyance.

"Why do you say 'I see'?
You don't see. *You understand.*"
The native Finn repeats his English-language question. I look
at my shoes, at the thousand faces of Vainamoinen.
The block is ambulatory, mutual.
I am a habit of speech, exigencies.
The sooty glass is brilliant and unreliable,
a glare in purgatory, a Vaselined wash.
The philosopher is in the garden; the telephone rings,
and the morning glories stand on the corner.
Dante scatters the distant women
in the monastic shimmer.

IV

It's marmalade in Alcatraz.
A beautiful indifference is let loose on a spree.
The lost pirate sings an Oriental song on the wrought-iron fire escape.
The glory of summer, suffused with orange day lilies,
counts each step on the road, the avian emigrant's address.
I hold a passport to my forehead. People pass through me,
the Queen of Sheba, high school girls.
They make me a crow. I feel their gentlest desire,
the mists of Benares.

A wristwatch of yellow birch on water
drifts near my nose. I am painting tiny portraits of weak emotions.
A black feather in a basket walks down a hill,
an affliction of vapors, dreamy *precieuses,*
fallen thorns: Western culture in a trivial drawing room.
Where is Fiordiligi? Where is this patch of ground?
The cane jaywalks, drips with rain.

Impunity sings to me. Too many syllables.
Minutes laugh with the oak tree leaves, ready-made mantras.
Dear Sampson, put one of your daughters on the phone,
one who mispronounces Egyptian words,
the "Swan of Tuonela," cow-headed, thirsty as hell.
The tongue is ceremonious, a geography of visual borders.
The lustrations of honey and oils
hum through a conch.

V

At the edge of an eyelid: Sibelius, cricket dew,
the electric jellyfish of sunlight, an ostrich in Heliopolis.
The snake of Thebes is useless,
a sistrum on a postage stamp of soil.
Between blades of the underworld, a human-headed wish
in the delirious thicket.
Our skin crosses the dark music,
the shoreline mathematical, serene.

A reverential silence devours the shade,
a slit in the bull's throat, and the jackals romp
in the stamen's glaze. The fish are terrible and hungry,
if the Jungians are right, and the pampas of Argentina has
never been softer, like tiny lizards in a maple tree.
One crow, feeling luxuriant, circles
the barometer. A wooden chair is wildly alive,
a pilot on the night river. Cupid leaves
cookies and milk for the archetypes,
a sweet spot in September.
How many lifetimes will the seal boy plunge?

VI

The cold spoons keep falling over,
hitting the school room. Pure murder, snack, snack.
The kid behind me sticks a pencil in a ticket.
The stones are compromised, spiritually blind, wrecked.
I stomped out of the drunk house, my head. Hello.
Lord Weary "brought me gladness to the grave."
My fingers unknot, daydreaming sharks in the shallows,
the reluctant cobalt a solace to the string quartet
of young days, not precisely Valhalla.

The big fat Buddha blinks like a mole,
no envy, incidently, for the goddamn bird watchers
who photograph the goddamn deer,
their bicycle rides, their tinctured butterflies.
The swallowed fishbone's fissures are secret
before eight o'clock in the morning.
Do you need fuel? Motes?

The kaleidoscope is innocent. Don't be
flip. The red insects come flying, solemn pleasures.
A chunk of quartz in the mineral bank eyeballs evolution.
Fatigue feels like hot tea. O Puer.
Bedtime, and we're sailing to a smoky island, the obvious
more florid than reality, which is too
"open" and "closed," too demi-monde.
Big sweating is best,
nestling lightly.

VII

The singsong light bulb—evasive, sublime.
It's only buzz. Plato's cavern is cloudy,
minute by minute a freaky gamble of glass marbles.
The troubadour, barefoot and fluttering, swims
in the irregular turquoise across the table,
the azure Mozart trapped in sensitivity,
in the ennui of the inamorata, the green kiss
without stars. Invisible color
in the atmosphere of a canoe.
I'm stuck. I'm swimming toward.

The crocodile is a Chevrolet, actual as flame,
and, today, you are Dolores Haze.
Nabokov's sad. The hurtling cars till the fairy tale,
and the parrot on your shoulder is a little stooped
in the Calypso, a strike closer, heavy freight.
The purple thistle is stagnant in the pool all day long,
"hasn't got a point of view," head bent
in smaller patience
like simian gazelles running a red light.

VIII

Wild perfume—Boo! Bulk!
Several blocks of Ellington, pedestrian rights
dipping like a swallow in the barn dusk:
inner drummings, possibility, the woman behind me
a prisoner awaiting sentence.
Some judicious nightforce that dust raises
becomes punctual, like strong hallelujahs,
and Donna Elvira walks within a veil,
an intimate sashay that suspects everything,
"so much motionless sound" O terra infidel,
your sudden clouds.

The creeping middle distance sits on a scarlet bench,
stopped in full flight, in murmuring patterns.
The sulking fugitive in the russet orchard
is diminished by "pallid innuendoes":
hold my wrench. The frost darkens.
Guess, guess, guess. The babyboomer hours,
consummate as charts of the world's darkest city,
crumble in an instant. The firmament falls into
my reedy heart, dropping fast. One needs
to be Lutheran. One needs not much.

IX

Osiris, god of contradictions,
the continual divorce is precarious.
The clock, the mind of a rational person, ticks,
lives in Vienna in a crazy museum, an hour with itself.
The spirit of weapons and musical instruments,
wildly needy, continual with distress,
smoked too much dope to speak,
and, still wounded, lifts its forehead out of this,
a villanelle, flapping like a torn sail.

Caravaggio isn't a dependable lover.
The light is awful this morning, a severe test
of irony, declining in age. Its name escapes me
like the process of definition, a man testing a plank.
Brazen sewing is a homely industry.
A devilish refrain smiles outwardly.
The concentration of colors flies apart,
Gipsy tints, studying the drama of Clyde Beatty
who has sighted Mexico at last,
a pink hurricane.

X

Smoke rings floated above Kafka and the cat was lying down.
I watched appearances abound, sad adults.
The harlequin masks were expensive, unshaven.
Their shadows flooded me as I looked toward the astral lava,
the gold flash of a whip, the face of my uncle.
The fables were too far away
in the shared cage.
The immigrant animals purred.
They called me Baby.

A money cup toppled him. He is so thin
in the middle of the sea, a sensate loom, unrecognizable.
The gorgeous miracles balanced on top
of a painted ball were a *comedie a tiroirs*, floodlit in the roar,
the raised bleachers glowworms above cotton.
There, the Duke of Mantua fought three leopards,
red, green and black as the studio of Matisse.
Wherever I look, the fear of coins rescues me,
like Beniamino Gigli in a bed sheet
on a white horse,
the fancy clothes of childhood.

XI

The harnessed satisfaction of an odd cobbler—
ordinariness with the eyes of a sheep
and the hindquarters of a dog—an exile
to the springs of strength (routinely a place
of ill-defined things), celebrates what appears to be
wooden, lifeless, bridled. I change a guitar string
and see an inherently narrative act:
kangaroos in a parking lot, atomized by Seurat.
There is nothing in front of me, nothing behind me.
The great eiderdown lions in "Peanuts"
fall through fractured glass,
alone at dawn.

A sleepy ancestor misses the red of life,
jogs closer to Tristan's sails, an abandoned garden
grey as a rain coat. Its featureless distortions shimmer.
Everyone is crossing Charon's river
with a civil nod. An elephant's ear floats,
disembodied, in the London fog. Great dead Greeks,
without a head, rear in the squinting pageant,
amended each April,
in the brilliance of middle age.

XII

"Finally," writes Apollinaire,
the opium spin-drift of Kiri Te Kanawa
makes erosion potent. The moon, with a boombox,
accosts De Quincey, devoured from the inside.
Every spice must pulse.
The sweet calculations of the old minister
shine, a prime number in the steep desert, "La Luna Asoma"
in the "Autumn Rhythm" of Pollock. Hand-blown
amethyst wakes early in a quick burst,
a pretty molten tassel.
The salmon threads of a kimono on oyster shells
shiver through a life-span in the fauve roll.
Borges walks the open plazas of Argentina.

Rhubarb,
its illimitable bursting prisms,
glinting in spasms near the evanescent toad,
pollinates the sublet. The riot and infirmity of duration
is post-aesthetic, imperfect bubbles trapped
in hazel blue. The silky wizened weather
gets to you, a pipe in the eye,
Jacques Barzun's spectacles, cherries.
The loam of boulders, iridescent ochre, flies.
A dozen varieties of lichen squeak and splatter.
Why isn't this simple? The scales of a dragon, zen minnows?
Snapped twigs in the puritan pines?

ANON

Tangled, inevitable,
the long-promised stage of life,
driven like a red Chrysler, genuinely terrifies
compromised women. When I lean down to the window,
a contingency both inside and outside the moment,
a hidden path rises up in the overflowing dawn.
I shift the caverns, the whirlwind of halos,
ferns swaying in the fun house
transformed from Basho
into a motion that coils. It's locked.
The advertisements are eternal and Freudian,
crowding the distractions of Brunhilde
on the passenger's side
my friend doesn't seem to hear.

In sign language, the bamboo grass
beside the rock-gathering orphan half smiles
and backs away on roller skates. In the rainwashed
gutter at twilight, Ithaca smells richly of lilac
and the mad noumenal limits of cognition
repress the lissome cars,
the sounds of cooking meat.
Pointing to my eyes, the ungainly shaking wings
Immanuel Kant could not bear
become concentric in the empty dales.
A thin apple branch radios the aberrations
just passing through the neighborhood.

When optics improved,
the displaced shrieking in the catalog,
aching to see a womanly profile,
identified a street sign,
refractory loops of whatever storm.
Edward Hopper is crisp in his starched navy uniform.
The Hibachi makes a kissing sound
in the vectors of inner dialogue,
and grey bits of hedgerows further suggest
the incomplete.
Unemployed leprechauns
read my application, clutching autumn trees.
Sweden is sepulchral,
"obliged to stick to possibilities"
gingerly.

VENDORS

"How fast can you type"
the overburdened fragility
of lonely widows in *tempo rubato*,
the hydrogen atmosphere bursting with sun spots
in the nurse's office, in the quickening
rock crystal of a "friendless" sensation?
Once, while clothed as a college Dean,
the planet, a dolorous vertigo of muscle spasms
in the middle of the day, lay in the dark, proofreading.
The quartz was cold, as if W. C. Fields fell asleep in a pool hall.
An out-of-body conference, devious in the stellar spectra,
dreamt of the Great Stone Mill.
Magellan was prepared,
driven to the floor by pain.

Some days (a title of civil dignity),
private hieroglyphs endure the moon-glow,
or a Roman soldier, or cracks in the wall.
No one knows why the sirens are silent.
Heraldic branches court authority:
a tuning fork in the month of March.
Archimedes traced the problem in the sand.
He abdicated, like Valentinus,
and followed the plumed head in the doorway
with his eyes closed, the cathedral's spawning rose
a roundel of meek distractions,
crowding the gloves.

Indian Summer

BURNISHED

You're better than Shakespeare, less
convoluted, profound. You're ineloquent,
cagey, limited, inwardbound. Shakespeare,
so wild, so searing, so stupendous, so tiring
's been done. A trillion dousing shadows continue
to trod upon the interlacing paragon,
Octavias adrift in Rommeling Egypts,
Pucks ascamper within the gargantuan felt-tip,
its careening convexities. You're more
personal than all the violining symphonies,
fifth, ninth, third, those immemorializing winds.
Libraries are slipping off
the edge of the earth, pages splayed, flapping, flapping,
brute brummagems, buckthorns, umber,
O androgen, Pluto's Bubo.
The glassy aquarelles are buoyant
above the buckra's bullworts. They watercolor
all the weevils, the whippets,
the whippletree's sonambulating picnics
with their aqueous soft-sell. They are blinkered and blowsy.
"If thy unworthiness raised love in me…"
They shun the wellaways. They wicker the snuffles.
They are *soigné*. Their solecisms saunter,
layering, erasing, then washing away
blustery aquamarine colors
in perambulating peaceful scenes, gradiant, giddy,
auroral, pretty. O see the yodelling billy-goated paintery
Innisfree, its incendiary hues: rice paper, mock orange, mustard,
the region's arpeggios' immersions—
"More worthy I…"

IMPRESARIO

"I hate these superwomen who tell
the government how they love
a small sand-fly sun,
thundering on stage: tense, light-footed,
rolling from wild peaks in the ironwood;
how their rushlight riverweed clavers,
'watches a bird fly until eyes become sky'
on essential margins,
with 'no real clothes—just astonishing earrings'
flickering on the rockbottom mesh,
'to make the world one household.'
Such 'edgy poise'
coils in the egg-shell echo.
It's enwreathing.
It bends the épée's stubborn thrust.
It equivocates the stud-poker ledgers
in the rear-view mirror's enormous glass road,
confusing the cooling
V-patterns of geese...
Shucks, the jam-packed icebergs boil—
steamy ejaculations.
Now that you've cooked me, eat me
atop a painter's palette."

LUNCH

His wife was out on errands,
arabesques, and his brain was pierced.
The eccentric sea's "gothic follies" bounced
in churning nonentities, garbled in glint.
The heart-qualming lukewarm twang of grasshoppers
sluiced the green arcades,
their flagrant palisades insolent.
The water rattled. Peek-a-boo. The argosy vexed.
A red-swatched laurel siren mayonnaised the horizon.
Middays demured
in the biscuited holograph,
in the ocean's buoyed solace.
The zooids mewed
in the menopausal spindrift,
the "smoky spoor light" libidinous.

FULL MOON

He hurls her through a window,
her eyes huge, brown, searing,
a burly, sun-scraped leveling against signs
of experience. A kind of febrile trance keeps arriving—
telecast, trumpeted, ceaselessly composing
brewed infusions of intermediary tasks.
Veiled opinions claim
cognizance at random in unearthed tarragon;
time, shrouded in musk, a stop action,
its mineralizing enamel frothy.

Sweeps of barren solitude
want cattle, green balconies, bowls of gruel—
hard-hatted ambassadorial images
so full of understanding about taxes.
Authentic touches stroke the great gray flank
where small porch lights
tumble toward peckerwood trustees.
Occasional cameras blush,
and cucumbers roil in the boilers.
The mechanized drifts of blackbirds
whip-saw the soliloquizing water moccasins
where the hobo's strawberry harvest
elevates brooks between chores;
a fusilade of hickory
doing floors again to make some money.

DIDJERIDOO

Troublemakers on the mule train
halt in the hothouse sunshine
as boyhood hours coil in the updraft,
resisting a brain drain.

Two Niagaras splutter in the yellow bunch grass
in a grove of self-educated persimmon.

A sunbaked ombu tree
tumbles through fields of soybeans.

MULCH

Between crystals that interconnect,
pockets of brine reflect
the monotony of perfection.
Newlyweds, busy working, don overcoats,
their oozing rainbows, in thumbworn opaque shrugs,
while the costumed priest,
with scabs the color of peaches,
asks "Where's my man?"
Waiting for missing links in the human chain,
quicksilver in thermometers,
("God gives, God takes away")
Naptown reels in the circuitous silence.
Hooligans, unshaded by trees, frown.
Bottles of soda pop sit in a refrigerator
near the bride's bedding,
carelessly strewn on thin margins
that immaterialize overdue dividends of desire—
the ambling cavalcades awaiting hay.
Downtown streets,
their weird solitude women-swept,
intone the fast-flowing sluggish red
of Baltimore's soul,
where man's early forebears, the australopithecines,
lacking culture, prowled
any green thing
fuzzed in pommelling yawls—
the liminal lateral shanty's blonding gongs
skittish castaways
in some domesticizing evensong.

HOPLITES

"Show me to my cabin
in Nyack, Biff," Doug said,
and suddenly shot across the salon.
On a nearby ridge, a fiberglass dinosaur in Dollywood,
trampled The Great Outside.
"May I tell you a disruptive truth?" Doug continued,
"Wittgenstein, serious-minded, his broadbeat
life zones spangling Odette
in slow curtain calls, crazy in the Biblical span,
upwinds the voracious oak, now the floorboards of Adonis,
dog-eared by ministrations of remorse,
and secures azured mania
in the providential rain-rich moss,
its elite quantums serrated, 'Worldsworthian,'
unprecedented, like kazoo'd kelp."

At this precise moment,
on mother-of-pearl, Svenn's nautical girl,
caught in claustrophobia, pliant, time-traveled, semi-nomadic,
jumps out of a truck for a sauna,
succinct in the matinee,
accosting looters imploringly,
at one with the aforementioned invertebrate
permafrosted in the javelin'd sky,
ambient, slaphappy.
"But Doug," Biff replies,
his beveled mini-van parked beside gospel timber,
"is she palpable as a sleeping child?"

RICE

Epauletted flunkies doorknob the Ramadas.
Absinthe'd pines whine and whine.
Rostropovich is serendipitous,
his evermores dizzy in synchrony: frangible convulsions
between tile-roofed rivers
where high-frequency weasels Buick the night.
An interruption,
an elf's beautiful chaos,
fills Eureka with soft vaporous light,
breaks bread with the sand rose.
Mammals sip goat's milk, as the echoing dodo swoons
like a pink pigeon trapped in sliding glass doors.
"As coach," Biff asks Doug,
"what's your strategy?"
After a decade, Doug's uniformed words return, in fatigues:
"Hippies fly in place, like red-spotted toads,
in auras of oncoming senility. My life is with my animals,
their complicated surf. Coyote transcendence
shields the eelgrass' mysteriously
vanishing embrace
long after simplistic cardboard patriots spawn."
Near the wreckage of a mobile home,
the wolf's rumble of rapids gophers each storm,
congealing scrims of tumbleweed
wives swish in *lau laos*
through the saw-toothed wall of winter.

BASKING IN BABYLON

The gamboling shells are fearful,
unemancipated on the squandered laugh-track,
in search of an "office" where they could be laid back,
patchy in the crustal sprawl,
daffodil'd, satirical,
among the port-holed paroxysms.

> *Zukofsky wrote Celia*
> *so many valentines.*
>
> *Their lives were entwined*
> *by his valentines.*
>
> *Celia, Celia, what did you say*
> *all that time?*

The dog-paddling declensions sway,
and the broom closet swings *amor patriae* your way, Oppenly.
The scarved boutiques zodiac the rummaged reefs.
Plunging bears, above, rove
the churched clingstone,
its rutilant sheen of caved sun downs,
while the fluted shells shoeshine the undertows,
all enmeshed inclemencies overthrown.

Under the flickflacking shrub's lionizing maw
is, and ever will be, the unsaid pulse.

AMTRAK

I

The trains are smokeless, the students eager to learn
about shoes: the possibilities of "balustrade," portraits
of parents, food. The car is in the pound, gathering money
for the city, its towed regulations towing me when I'm
too entranced to read signs. My mother waits in Washington,
her birthplace, for "Dardy," her firstborn in that marbleizing
gloam of the military, its thrusting obelisk encircled by
Old Glories, its huge entombing statues quipped with memorial
speeches struck in stone. Obviously alone, sipping coffee
with Hopper on red linoleum near "Joe Louis Drive," I'm wired,
wavelengthed with the dimmed radio'd songsters who Muzak
these coffeeshop skies. It seems there's nowhere inside,
streetwise, without them. I miss the silencing meadows,
those wickered picnics one sees in films, in "Enchanted
Aprils." A bus, mirrored behind Rice Crispies and pineapple
juice cans, slatters through my head in this Hopperland.
My mother will meet me where The White House rests
flatly in reality, not unlike Doonesbury. It's 8:00 am. Forks
break up the scrambled eggs. Toast, seared by Ad Reinhardt,
floats in a saucer of coarse porcelain at the repast of
an old man seated nearby "Better with Coke" dispensers.
Too much tobacco smoke weaves through the Whitney.
It separates me, the eye myopically stilled. The museum's
huge elevators rise to Duncan's lover's many rooms,
their complicated collages.

II

Jersey's snaking freeways, propped by beige dragon legs
reflected in petrochemical lakes, stapled by phone poles,
bury me alive in bright factory daylight. Acura billboards
rise: "Some Things are Worth the Price." Newark's proud
downtown gleams behind the slumped river's colorless tides.
Hopper peeps inside the train station's Waiting Room where
purpled slate faces move through gray glass. "Wannakeepit?"
placards spy on the pit stop, a momentary clustering
of tropes, signifying "Tony's Truck Tires" to come in the
bumptious glide. The fevered eye alights, with thankful
hollowness, upon the comfort of ugly architecture, the
glad-rag traintrack trees of October, the occasional flaming
("I am that which is becoming") bush. The snack car is
lap-topped now, the gin-rummy boozers historic; sloshed Harley
T-shirt guys a memory. I miss their silver-skulled fists, their
preening sadness and disheveled baseball-capped hair. They'd
never reach the front door in Singapore, its whip-lashing barbers.
Where are they? In trucks? In beat-up cars? Gone from
"Playland's Kiddyland Rides," the static signs on Track Four,
gone from Railfone, another new word, "Entering Edison."

III

The swishing quickens. Olivegreen trees blur me.
The mind expires, gladly, tired of *samizdat.* An oppression
rattles the trance. Power is destroying me, my own. I
need evaporating release, "Walker Gordon Milk," "Good
Friends Chinese Restaurant." I isolate in innumerable
bark trunks, their cluttering sunstruck array. I isolate
in fright. The past inhumes the brain, yakking. Oh, the
brightest white water tower rises, an Oldenburg thimble
in the flushed wild rust. Ordinary cars scar the brief vision:
"Basket Case Inc." To think and not to think, to watch
television, to visit and avoid Washington at the same time,
to take my mother to Granny's Maryland, the Potomac
homestead, and feel, as she so wishes to be, rooted, her
"Colonial Dames" hotel meetings one of her bewildering
connections (unlike me, my parents believed in this country).
Pride, twists from within to turn, daggered by light,
outside. "Wanted Owner Operators." "Hit Me with a Sunbolt."
Hopper's columns re-enclose Philadelphia's escalators,
receedingly. The shocked sun's clarity encoils Bower Field
Stadium, Penn Tower. A green truck, stuck in the net of
a white spider, now rests on sheltering concrete as the net
breaks and breaks on the tracks' quake, its dried banks
of dirt, its distancing injestions, the dumb flat buildings'
Stella'd facades near "Suh's Baby City," a fallingdown shop
in everyman's urban slum. "The woods decay, the woods
decay and fall" in firesome autumnal squalls. Huge circular
fuel tanks are Smithson's thumb prints, now Wilmingtons
away. Oscar, we must have tea. Walker Evans is following
me. Paris is so unfair.

THE SEA FLOOR'S BROKEN PLATES

Partly blasé in social calendars,
a recalled child webbed in forty-seven skeletons,
Odette swirls in the purple-and-black
anarchy, her plastic rosary
wormholed, sweltering, breathtaking
in the catapulting grottoes,
the ventriloquistan whorlwinds.
Liquors distilled from sugarcane cackle in the fever,
too early for church. The quizzical gondola's
capsized loops recombine in the steamy telenovela,
as the communal cornfields, shawled by roosters,
lace-ruffle her womanhood.
In clattering pantries where Archimedes wept
above blood puddings,
their transubstantiations backlashed
across the Acropolis in jackhammered slats,
a prayer, an afternoon,
envelopes the expiring tutu
in the heavenwarding stagecraft,
the consequenting centennials of vaudeville,
touseled to exhaustion,
in the hazardous inflammable fathoms
of the danceworld's dish.

COURTING

The gavelocks churr,
and the illuviun morning cicatrizes the bluing sabbath,
enamored by everything, content.
The coral bells aloft,
in cracked tempura,
are nudged by breadroot as Icarus sails
safely above the twink of twinflowers in a turnabout cloud shower.
The tullibees bleep
and the rosaniline tundra, once so dry,
slinks into the scrumbled sea,
the scrieving flowstone screwy, as usual.
Funky scruples that make people cry will be ribald tonight.
So much occurs in the rosewood's
reverberant groundswell, in the ripsaw bays.
The rhyme comes on time. The rockoons fly,
assurgent, plumed.
The jousted ring lifts upon the lance,
the lady's ribbons flow
downward to meet the dark-hoofed
curtsy.

LANGUID LARGESSE

At the crowded *café terrasse*—
video'd powwows spreading silver
through tricky channels—the Thousand Islands folk,
inbound entrepreneurs,
coax the sea's crunch of gravel
in alabaster dinghies
through conservative grays.
The laconic, river-running sun,
assuages the low profiles,
as the oxeye'd daisies' rugged trumpeting breaks apart the lake,
the wintering swans beneath the sky's skull
a maroon moraine.
The bare jawbone of musclemen,
their chestnut moorings separated from the earth,
are modest artifacts among the unchieflike consoling rocks.
Black-and-white cockerspaniels
paw the inky silence Herodotus harnessed
in suspended pastures of white gauze,
its intercepted twinge
an appliqué of lissome devotion
—cobwebs, cedar nuts, steppe cats—
by dint of mythical curios,
to the pregnant male,
to the seahorse's dating service
expelled in spurts,
the palomino sea grasses' lodestone inference.

MARTINI AT THREE

I felt little, I felt tough, I felt funny.
School was accommodating: tetherball, jocks.
A teacher who limped from polio
was kind, Miss Somebody in Schoffield Barracks
in the fifties in elementary Hawaii. She taught me
the word "magnificent." College
was less lucky: a lifelong alteration,
the perception of misery, failed posture tests,
profs secretly sodomized by profs,
so my old tutorial gentleman honors adviser
told me, ten years later, when I visited him and his wife, Esther,
who spent their waking lives indexing Victorian literature.
He found me less intelligent than different.
He spent time with me, silver-swept, elegantly.
We met in the mausoleum'd library,
its strange bookish engagements awesome,
talked Browning,
the flush of an available God,
before William Morris' brittled roses
broke apart the devoted heart of bedrooms,
before Hardy's tearless taut elegies, before Maud,
before Viv, her slow mendicant disintegration,
and, then—martinis, martinis, martinis,
thoughtless power, quick, transcendent, sure,
suffering abolished like a sentimental tossaway—
who needs feelings, anyway?
Speed clicks,
throws away the key.
Martinis, their consumptive unfatal tragedy,
they had to go.
The details are unspeakable, frankly.

44

SLUSH

Unmoored coordinates
play second fiddle to bedrock.
The lantern is green, and the supernovae are sandstone
at the bottom of the tureen. All is
reliable in the slanting phosphorescence
where algebra is alluvial.
The terra incognita is veined, benumbed,
her soul so many corrigenda.
They ermine her patios
and blur in responding softness the pewlike malls,
the doe-eyed cars' metallic pastels,
the Santa shoppers' spiky holly with beads so pretty
in the snow's aberrant agendas,
paling the self-serve pumps, their pirouetting
numerals aflow in an Ed Ruscha photo.
Latency becomes a cloven-hoofed
crescendo. All is there in the deadpan air,
each pizza logo leisured in the upholstery of motion;
or, as Marjorie would say, "the geology of the situation"
is salient. But sleep, that cloudy incumbent,
calls—habitual, preeminent,
and slow-mo's each flown allegro.
Sleep with me, the snow falls so many times.

MASS

In the crude gristmill
taunting the gypsy moth's continual selves,
the sun's corona
rings
the squirrel fish
and the extravagant dimension liquifies.
So nice a day to be inside.

GABLES

                    Some wives just like
            somebody else driving,
                keeping time to the swishing music of skis,
                            the Orpheus-ascending waterfalls,
                    the rare and lonely call
                            of the lorikeet.
            A primitive aura of valor,
        "flesh the texture of a reed,"
                        sweeps their clangorous trepidations,
                    lovingly, as a pocket comb,
            nervous in the "fog-soaked extremities,"
                            repeats its unhurried waverings —
                "glancing rivulets"
                        "in the decoy mess of a dream."
                    So many touchés diverge in the asylum'd sonata—
            "the crêpe harbor"—that contains foozled shards.
    There, wives become flummoxed
                        localized, inparticular;
                    but, Oh, these cross-stitched skies
            that collide and collide
                    swoom merely in a husband's shadow, so tell.
                    The church bell's melees,
                unlatch, rolic
        these lusters, dainty in light conversation, ilex-ushered,
                to the one who sees you through
                            the pterodactyled fortnights,
                    their yearning flummeries,
            to the comma'd croo, twixt coo and croon,
                the silken locomotion
                            of you.

LITTLE TRIPS

Just as I was about to do my monthly invoices
to continue to earn my living in order to pay quarterly estimates
in support of city services—subways, medics, mimes—
John's "Philosophy of Life" arrived,
questioning everything.
It answered nothing except some yearning
for sand-flown bare toes on the seaward dunes,
the dream of a lover in front of me, sandy,
Bobby Kennedy touch football dressed, maybe,
shaggy, lumbering down happily to the dollared shores,
someone I could care for, be around,
as if Sagaponack existed only in February
and the crabs, solemnized in blooped holes,
were pleased, smug in their eye-blinked kingdoms
where the sun above rolls on pale blue Freilicher scrolls,
and the sky is so wide and quiet.
My invoices stayed, paper clipped in place, delayed,
on the far side of my mind, even though I knew I must
get paid or I couldn't work in the city
and help the avenues to be repaved,
the potholes repaired, finally.
I floated all morning in John's philosophy.
The quieting windows, their millennia of brick,
were sunny, bright in the postmodern October
of yesterday, as if a cerulean train
just passed by and, through glass sand,
John waved.

HELIOTROPE

A sunflower in the psychomesh,
Clytie, once a water nymph, swoons in reticence,
her bold abeyance watchful. She is bathed and bathed,
but lonely in her petaled enclave,
her salamandering hours
enslaved to daylight.
The goddess Diana races past her, Diana,
restless with gruff thorned speed, fast flicking ferrets at her feet.
A bright vacuity alights upon Clytie,
her ewe-eyed stare fixed with such constancy,
ovine in the panicky woodsmoke,
primal, dogged, cogent.
Her absentminded Apollo leers
above his cannonading steeds' revolving violets
that sprawl upon the army-blanket trees
in screeds of dusks,
Apollo, gnarled by his own ambering compliance,
his reign-clenched responsibility.
A flare, a mute floozy, in the raven-ruddered night
is Clytie, the sunflower's rounding ever-patient loyalty.
She brims in the orange calvary,
manacled to the piebald eons,
her strained pressure meekly orbiting,
as if forever weeping from the quarter-mooned
windborne ground.

PARCHED

The inability to speak,
the ground swell's oblique terrain, the racing
camel's hoofbeat that becomes, in depressions of sand,
dromomania upon
wind-swished inclines of land,
outrides leisurely time,
as if brine had no mermaid weaving in the oceans below,
no roustabout to greet the loam, no red slippers
to don, to twirl,
for the one she once saw
from her moist, surf-struck sea rock
where she dared to gaze, sea locked in tidal strategems,
amazed. Her calling fellatios
fail in the fearful structure of space.
She is a fairytale, statue in the North Sea, a curio
cast in metal, that boats with awnings pass.
And, all the while, the etiolating sands,
their widening *personae gratae*, hush and hush
the slippers' dance, that red moment in fairyland,
its gyral vagaries,
for the *sotto voce* runes, bleached by *amour fou,*
the roweled sand-sapient crossings,
their waterless waftures breaking and breaking
across scorched parlays to link,
oasis to oasis,
those, in this errant conveyance,
who stammer, trembling to drink.

SOUTH

With theorems arcane as lamé
worn gracelessly at a power brunch
and Apalachicola Bay tucked away
in geography, where it belongs, most say,
its hoteliers still receiving personal checks
from strange guests —Yankees, dust catchers, naiads—
the burrs' convergence
remains understaffed; but,
lookit, geezer, the apogee's still a balmy spot
where parodists unveil the juggernaut
and the *aurora borealis* blinks frequently, does it not,
in Saturday's phantoming cultures
where drum-rolling Titans hold "unlimited meetings."
I need to get friendly. The puce rust,
its stumbling yesteryears mere fribble,
has stained the periscopic view,
the "green linoleum," too.
Houses boomerang in the heat, clashing colors,
and there are more endings than there used to be, muzzy ones.
They bedraggle the toga's starlight,
its simian milieu,
and make late night a cauterized sinew.
The quiescence is queer,
"Enjoy'd no sooner, but despised straight..."
I need you. Oops, the table is breaking down.
The brunch people stare.
Apalachicola is everywhere.

CONSUMED

The propelled confusion's clean sheets
brandish confinement,
remunerations of stiff friction
a necessity,
but those lavendar triumphs
are previous,
carboned, apocryphal,
an Alioth's factory.
Tattoos on a shoulder are more reliable,
and I believe the juggernaut recedes
with labelling.
Implicity unfolds,
relaxes.
Your hand creams
sweep me out of sight,
a tracer in chilly scar light.

EAVES

These fretful conferences
while shopping for sneakers
in the balmy inertia,
the barnstormed commodities giddy in the faint heat,
leave me
browsing reality,
its cockamamie interpass
swooshed by bootstraps,
and wondering if continuity
overissues class,
if all knees may meet in these
disorienting pews.
I'm nosy and variants soothe me
as if the pulse were flung outside the body,
could be observed
in the peppercorn world
which is waylaid omnipresent
before the mumbling laity. Have you heard
me or are you double parked again,
unable to enjoy the city,
its turnstile nightgowns on Madison's mannequins,
the Banana Republic's ephemeral linens?
For goodness sake, meter the car
and come in. I want to try
on a shoe salesman.

Queries

YO, BRO'

I'll mesh men with your women.
The desert is vacuous and its twirling grids
earwax the nervous system.
Quarrels are beautifully colored
upon the lawless reservoir of patience,
the flustering soft tediums in the underwater tapdance,
its relapsing evasions.
The cursive backdrop indents,
its vocalise jolly and black,
but you are too Transylvanian for that,
the flip-card news opportune;
too Cagean. I quibble with these schemes,
their quilting tears uninvolving.
The pudding kingdom is a crowded dorm,
its watery radios delinquent.
The facile crayfishing jerks.
Too many photostats gag the oracle
until homelife blurs, and sophistication,
its essay-like stains, jet-skis
blundering piquancies
over all the Ouija's bordering claims.

DIVESTITURE

I buried the chopsticks
under The Star Spangled Banner,
careful to confuse
the fruit-flavored scientists,
their collective rumors
tearing the flesh;
but the novel called it "peace,"
and the blue-blotted women
riled in numberless waves, latently,
while a blur kissed the knitted miracle,
too weak to unbutton the rules.
I touched the enslaving nylons,
their casualizing torrents
chaste as drowning diction,
and felt intensely tough-minded
for a minute, as if I could be
minimally medieval, shocked, biological,
the flag itself a rippling breast,
but junk mail modulated the streaked system
and the bluegrass tutus blanked.
My masculinity's so awkward
and, Lord knows, locution's cursory,
its petty hail a continent.
Silky doodles of thread
Betsy Ross my head, porn me slack.
I'm dexterously impotent, 'n all that.
I think I'll color the evidence green.

WHITEWALLED

The *a priori* debutantes wince,
hobble upward in steadfast seasons of space,
their juicy austerity bony,
sequestered amid the messy obbligatos,
their faithless do's and don't's.
The ochre moon's reflection,
its catalog of carrots and swallowed owls,
husks the hand grenades scattered upon the ground,
their lambent uselessness
woodpeckered,
and illuminates the sleepy pickpockets
in burrowed foxholes,
their pet food dreams harpooning the pantyhose.
A padding overweening
the opaque scene, feverishly,
and the neon intercourse vexes the flowers
in the beekeeping musk.
Denial and martyrdom, how they tremble,
the duelling eyebrows
lacquering flames.
Let me explain this disruption.

URGENT

Those nuclear nipples spooned in the hunchbacked hills,
Santa's harems, still deliver,
the treadmills of turkeys above
ever secure. Long baths
lavish the attagirls, dilute soft flesh frankly.
War, for a strange reason, subsides
within the linoleum-like porcelain tiles,
steamy Chiclets.
The curtseying generations,
their spoolish spin,
educate missiles with muzzling disinterest,
but each hulking breeze
denies sovereignty
and smudges compactors with feeling.
Hot water, please,
my toes need its purring relief.
I am someone's sweetheart maneuver.
Under me are such silos.
They squeeze themselves through clover.

SNUG

Messiahs, maledictions, men...
oh, when will the candelabras converge
and the pacemaker's shuddering phosphorous
particle the ocean-looped earth,
cummberbund The Second Coming?
Privilege prevails, and the deltas reconvene,
undefeated. The divisible table talk
outwriggles each wrist. No one can name
the larva's uterus or wish
the world credentials.
Beavers with sideburns
trip the ploughs.
The rose garden's nomenclature ruffles.
The immense hmmmmm accelerates,
and the hand-held voltage salutes.
I am colonized,
touch me gently,
I have overspent the loam's destiny,
its colorless stamina
stoic. I witness alternating thievery,
the embryo's ventilation
immuring me within
a yippee's last hallucination.

Dissolving

SCULPTING IN TIME

I met a painter without a penny,
a sculptor, a steelfarer, a Marine in Danang,
a drug-runner. I gave him two subway tokens
and bought him several dinners.
I rested on his shoulder and he told me
about Dorothea Richardson. Men always know
things: Tarkovsky quotes. He wanted to be wild
and messed up, a familiar feeling. He wanted to be cared for
by a good woman, a sweetheart. I saw it all coming,
love, generosity, the keys to my car.
I saw the whole struggle humming before me,
proximity, compromise, the usefulness of money,
so empty in the moribund bank,
bereft of slashed steel-framed abstracts,
that I was born an angel to this man.
We fought. I told him to minimum wage part-time,
enough dinner checks had been tipped
from my side; that generosity
would unwind the shouldered repose
and the shutters would close, but he needed
dinner. He is out with his dinner now, her turn.
I hesitated and my heart is unburned.
Does this make me sagacious? I am so tired of wisdom.
I am placed. I've paid my mortgage.

I sit alone, sore throat. Brokers lose my savings.
They want big trades, commissions,
smooth-talk to clients who are women. It happens.
People get by. Burns are safe in the miraculous lamplight.
"Experience is a euphemism for failure," Emerson said.
Old notebooks fall on my head. Nothing is new.
I think of you, removed from all this,
an evapotranspiration, an evening primrose.
Windows are scared of windows,
their ricocheting views.
We could have a cup of coffee. I could pay for you.

SARAH'S COMMUNIONS

Above Marie's rugs,
the celestials are soft and white.
The Princess Kaiulani room is spare
in the fluorescent twilight where lights climb
up rectangular spines as if, as Wilde mused, Niagara
Falls surged upside down. You say again
you don't know what you will do,
your upsy-daisy plans made out of the blue,
rich wives lending you purchased furniture, painted chairs,
accoutrements for the ghost writer
who makes famed men wiser,
their lives retyped in the loving memoir
you devise, their warbly texts rechecked and chastised,
the historic culture of their times smoothed,
exhumed by faithful anonymity.
Have Tolstoys always kept a secretary
to transcribe huge minds, matching verisimilitude
with devotion? The hidden kitchen
in the off-white lofted room has no coffee,
no need for easy stimulation. The heart moves
the computer keys until the back is cramped on Sundays.
Money is made and saved. All your debts are paid,
the future evanescent as a Makapuu wave,
its deep blues winterized and rolling.

Friends, furtive travelers, drop in, disordered by life.
They swim in your decades like drum-rolled fish,
seeking clarity in the watery mesh,
attenuation.
Your West Virginian cat is solarized in safety
where your brother continually befriends a lovely heiress
and farm animals spackle invaluable views.
When your work is done, I will remember you,
your signature forever deleted from the histories you renew,
your breath, your upright spellcheck, your belief
in what others do.

REDEEMER

The beautiful church bells, how easy they spell
relief. Their clinking melodies ping between
the mechanized roaring of Laguardia's planes,
the muffled honking of the streets,
an Armenian consulate footfalls
away, the withering weed-trees at bay,
sheltering truckloads of deliveries. Each day,
at noon, church bells enter the living room
as if I lived in the steepled childlike grid
of a Grandma Moses countryside
where bricks were stacked from without rather than within,
laid to make quaint house walls by the town's masons
instead of invisibly seaming elevated halls.
The bells, some shepherd's flute re-tuned in swells,
drift through the smoggy latitudes,
enter November's crack in the overcast window,
the sky pale as basin detergent,
white and powdered, a scrubbed tub above.
No sooner heard, the tonal interruptions,
the bells' melodies, used with words in ordinary hymns
played on the family piano during austere gatherings
in spare candle-lit cabins, cease,
leaving, like a jetstream, a presence,
a reminiscence, something once, and still, believed.

ACKNOWLEDGEMENTS

The epigraph for *October for Idas* consists of two pages from my grandmother's book, *The Classic Myths in English Literature and Art* by Charles Mills Galey, Ginn and Company, Boston, 1911. It is inscribed: "Margaret B. Williams, S. F. C. Petersburg, Va., 1912." For "Portrait of Steve," I am deeply grateful to the poet Steve Kuusisto for permitting me to collage from the early prose drafts of his memoir on his experience of going blind as an adult. The words and images in this section are his; they have been lifted out of context, altered, and rearranged into different lines. Some of the poems in "Indian Summer" are collages fashioned from the novel *Time Remaining* by James McCourt, John Ashbery's *And The Stars Were Shining*, Derek Walcott's *Omeros,* George Oppen's "Daybooks" in *Ironwood 26*, and Louis Zukofsky's *ALL: the collected short poems*. In the poem "Slush," the phrase "the geology of the situation" alludes to Marjorie Welish's poem "Grace's Tree I" in her book *Casting Sequences*. The section "Queries" was inspired by three books by Bruce Andrews: *Moebius, Divestiture – A*, and *I Don"t Have Any Paper So Shut Up (or, Social Romanticism)*. The poem "Sarah's Communions," in the last section, is for my childhood friend from Honolulu, the playwright and novelist Sarah Fagan Lewis. My thanks, also, to the Virginia Center for the Creative Arts and Blue Mountain Center for their generous support.

Peggy Eliot

Star Black was born in Coronada, California, and was raised in Washington D.C. and Hawaii. She holds degrees from Wellesley College and Brooklyn College. She is the author of two books of poems, *Double Time* (The Groundwater Press), and *Waterworn* (Tribes Books). She works as a photographer and visual artist based in New York City.